Chicken Poop in my Bowl

101 Jokes & Stories To Lift The Spirit And Crack A Smile

WRITTEN & COMPILED BY

John M. Irvin

Chicken Poop In My Bowl

John M. Irvin
Lifestyle Enhancement Services, Inc.
Copyright©MCMXCVII

Printed in the United States of America.

Cover design and text layout by Ad Graphics, Tulsa, Oklahoma 800 368-6196

ISBN: 0-9656428-0-1

Published by:

J & C Publishing
P. O. Box 4397
Tulsa, Oklahoma 74159-0397

Order Information
To order more copies of this book or to receive a
complete list of other products by John Irvin
contact:

Lifestyle Enhancement Services, Inc.
by calling toll free:

1-888-997-PHUN

Dedication

This book is dedicated to my beautiful, loving wife and partner, Cindy. The encouragement and constant prodding with which she has provided me has earned her the official business title of: **Cindy Irvin, P.M.S.**, that's Professional Marketer of Spouse, and, believe me, she has earned both, the initials and the title!

I love you, Cindy.

Here's The POOP

Introduction

Chicken Poop in my Bowl

"I just can't remember jokes!"

This is probably the most often heard phrase wherever I do my Hilarity Therapy® programs and seminars. Perhaps you have said this line yourself. If you have, don't feel like you are all alone. Approximately 98% of all the people in our society feel that they can not remember and tell jokes well. Only 2% believe that they can! And most of these people's spouses will disagree.

(By the way, did you know that 98% of all statistics are made up right on the spot?)

So chances are, this book is in the hands of someone who may feel that he or she can not or does not remember jokes well. Someone, perhaps, like you. Maybe that's the case. Maybe not.

In Hilarity Therapy®, I have told people time and time again the secret in remembering jokes. "When you hear a joke, jot it down! I mean, how do you remember anything else? You take notes! Perhaps just a few key words will suffice. But you put pen to paper and just this act alone will help to stimulate your cerebral matter and increase your ability to remember. So treat a joke like anything you wish to remember. Take a few notes."

I've said this over and over. So finally I thought to myself, "John, why don't *you* write the jokes down. Write them down and put them in a book. That way, when someone comes up to you and says, 'I don't remember jokes!', you can say, 'Buy this book!'"

All of the jokes in this book are *real!* Yes, these are *real* jokes! I did not make any of these jokes up. These are jokes that I have heard from others, many others. Some of these people I remember, and some, I do not. I heard these jokes at conferences and at conventions. I heard them at movies and in shopping malls. Some I gathered at soccer games, and others, while on the phone. Some I heard in bathrooms, and some in hospitals. Some jokes came from strangers and some from friends (who I believe just may be stranger yet!). Some jokes I heard many different times, all from totally different individuals. Some of these jokes, I have embellished and changed around a bit. Many I did not, but kept them in their purest form.

I've tried my darndest to keep from upsetting, embarrassing or making angry, anyone. I have attempted to use only the finest of joke material, and to weed out anything offensive. You have no idea how many jokes I eliminated from these pages due to their adult nature. (Of course, this could make up a whole other book, *Chicken Poop in the Adult Bowl*, just let me know what you think!)

But, with the nature of jokes, most will ridicule someone. So I just want to caution you, you might be offended. If you offend easily, I have included a list below of all persons or groups that are mentioned in these pages. Simply read through the list and if you see something mentioned with which you are of delicate nature, be cautious. I have tried to provide equal opportunity, and equally offend all, by doing my best to be non-offensive to everyone. As Joel Goodman says, "I can tell the same joke to three different people, one will be laughing his head off, the second will say, 'I don't get it', and the third will be totally offended."

So here's the list and lighten up!

Joke brunts:

Doctors, lawyers, secretaries, bosses, mothers, fathers, clergymen, genies, bears, hikers, golfers, policeman, dead people, Baptists, Methodists, Catholics, birds, ancient kingdoms, Alexander the Great, timekeepers, communists, cats, flies, Elvis, baseball, funerals, drug stores, judges, cruises, light bulbs, home owners, psychiatrists, Californians, Texans, Oregoneons, male chauvinists, blondes, divorced males, little guys, big guys, cowboys, waitresses, senior citizens, kids, Jesus, bulls, vegetables, string, cats (did I say cats already?), dogs, clones, teachers, deep sea divers, department stores, married people, yo-yo's, drunks, cannibals, engineers, animal rights activists, people with glass eyes, ophthalmologists, goats, boys, farmers, first aid, getting older, neurotics, HMO's, abuse, evangelicals, potatoes, Dan Rather, dads, poodles (not to be confused with dogs), self-improvement courses, complainers, O.J. and the justice system, gassiness, loan officers, truck drivers, penguins, pirates, computer programmers, Siamese twins, frogs, the Bobbitts, turtles, Irishmen, unfaithful spouses, vagabonds, innkeepers, politicians, wildlife officers, endangered species, yuppies, the unemployed, and myself.

If I've left anyone out, please let me know and I will include you in my next book.

1

A Hoosier Hike

There's an old Indiana story that tells about a Great Bear and a Furry Rabbit who happened to be traveling together. Little is known of their relationship prior to this destined journey.

So on this one Great Journey, Great Bear and Furry Rabbit were hiking along this particular Hoosier trail. Bears and Rabbits have terrifically fibrous diets, you know, and they were exercising heavily. This combination of elements caused and promoted the contractions of their intestinal tract. It wasn't long before they felt a particular urge, that one urge with which one is so particularly delighted, especially with advancing age. They were great hikers and knew the courtesy of the trail. They stepped well off the path and into some bushes. They scraped away a scrap of topsoil and stooped to a squatted position.

Nature was having her way. Our friends and heroes admired their surroundings alive with birds and all of God's living creatures.

Great Bear turned to Furry Rabbit and asked in a Great Voice, "I'm wondering, Furry Rabbit, you're so sleek and so soft. I'm wondering if I might ask you a rather delicate and personal question."

Furry Rabbit looked up at Great Bear, he felt rather startled. He felt they were good friends and no doubt thought it odd that Great Bear would ask such a question.

Furry Rabbit answered in his meek and nervous voice. "Great Bear", he squealed, "we're good friends and please, ask your question."

Great Bear lowered his booming voice, "I'm wondering if you ever have... the problem," he hesitated.

Furry Rabbit said, "Go on Great Friend. Ask your question."

"Well," the Bear began again, "Do you ever have the problem... of poo... sticking... to your sleek fur."

Furry Rabbit giggled, "Why no." He chuckled. "Of course not." He giggled again.

Great Bear looked down for a moment, pensive, and looked back at Furry Rabbit. And his Great Voice boomed, "GOOD!"

Great Bear then picked up Furry Rabbit, wiped his great behind and set Furry Rabbit back on the ground.

2

Ain't No Bull

Two men were crossing a meadow while on vacation in Idaho. Suddenly, from across the field, they heard the bellowing and the thundering of hooves as a huge bull came charging towards them.

One of the men was lucky enough to head for a nearby tree and climbed its limbs to safety. The other, however, did not spot the tree and headed off toward the opposite end of the meadow. The bull took after him.

The man realized that he would never make it to safety when he spied a large hole just ahead to his left. He veered to the left and dove into the hole just as the giant bull would have reached him. The bull leaped over the hole and turned about. The man came up out of the hole. The bull charged again and the man leaped back into the crevice. Once again, the bull jumped the spot as the man came back up, and the bull charged once more, their actions were repeated.

"Stay in the hole, you fool, stay in the hole," his companion shouted from the safety of the tree.

"Fool, yourself!" cried the man, as he scampered once more from the hiding place, "there's a bear in that hole!"

3

Amen

Then there was the evangelical minister who rehearsed and rehearsed and rehearsed each and every sermon, over and over and over again. You see, he really practiced what he preached.

4

An Eternity

An attorney was talking with God. He asked God thoughtfully, "God, what is a million years like to You?"

God said, "A million years? Oh, it's like a second!"

The attorney started to think along a certain line and asked, "God, what is a million dollars like to you?"

God answered, "A million dollars? Oh, it's like a penny."

So this attorney now is really thinking and he thinks that maybe he can make something here. So he asks, "God, will you give me a penny?"

God said, "Sure. In a second."

5

Bar One

A little mushroom went into a bar. He slid up onto the bar stool and asked politely, "May I get a drink, please?"

The bartender answered gruffly, "No, we don't serve your kind in here."

"Why not?" the mushroom inquired. "I'm a fungi."

6

Bar Two

The little sandwich went into a bar. He slid up onto the bar stool and inquired, "May I get something to eat?"

The bartender looked down at the little sandwich and answered, "No! We don't serve food here!"

7

Briefs

Do you know how to get a lawyer out of a tree?

Cut the rope.

• • •

What do you call 3000 lawyers at the bottom of the ocean?

A good start.

• • •

What do you say to an attorney with an IQ of 40?

Good morning, your honor.

8

Daiquiri Night

Two boys were best of friends, Dick and James. They were in the same grade school, middle school and high school together. Even though they went to different colleges and took up different professions, they remained close. Upon completion of their studies, Dick and James both returned to their small town to begin their careers. Dick was now an attorney, while James had studied medicine and was now a general practitioner.

When they returned to the small town, they decided that they would meet each Friday night just to keep in touch and keep their ongoing friendship alive and current. So every Friday at 6:00 pm, James, the doctor, would arrive at Dick's, the attorney's, place. Dick, in celebration would have a blender of almond daiquiris ready and waiting. So on Fridays, they would drink, laugh and tell each other the happenings of the previous week's work.

This had been going on for quite a long time, when one Friday afternoon, Dick opened his cupboard to find that there were no almonds. "Goodness," he thought, "what am I going to do? Doc will be here soon and there are no almonds!"

As he looked through all his cupboards and cabinets, he was dismayed to find no almonds. However, in one drawer, he came across a small unopened package of some hickory nuts. Dick had never made daiquiris with hickory nuts before, but how different could they be? So following his original recipe, only substituting the hickory nuts for the almonds, Dick proceeded to produce a luscious blender full of daiquiris.

Six o'clock arrived just as James the Doc drove into Dick's driveway. It had been a long week and the Doc was anticipating that first daiquiri with pleasure. He hurried from his car up the sidewalk and he let himself in, Dick promptly handed him a tall icy glass which he immediately placed to his lips and eagerly began to drink. A look of confusion came across his face.

"Dick," he asked, "Is this an almond daiquiri?"

"No," answered Dick, "It's a hickory daiquiri, doc!"

2

Death By Drowning

Old man O'Reilly had worked down at the local brewery for years. Then, one day, he wasn't paying close attention as he walked the walkway above the giant beer vat. He tripped, lost his footing, and fell directly into the vat and drowned. The supervisor thought that it should be his duty to relay the tragic news to O'Reilly's widow.

He went to O'Reilly's house and rang the doorbell. When Mrs. O'Reilly answered the bell, he told her of her husband's demise.

"I'm sorry to tell you, Mrs. O'Reilly," he said, "but today your husband fell into the beer vat and drowned."

"Oh my!" she exclaimed. She wept and wept and covered her face with her dish towel, trying to muffle the agonizing sobs. After a bit, she asked, "Tell me, did he suffer much?"

"I don't think he did," the foreman explained. "He climbed out of the vat three times to go to the men's room!"

10

Due Respect

The foursome was out on a beautiful Saturday afternoon. Everything was perfect and they were having a terrific game. At the seventh hole, Bob was just about to take his swing, when a funeral procession drove by on the nearby street. Bob stopped his swing, removed his cap, held it over his breast and looked down, silently.

The other three were in awe, when one remarked, "Bob, I never knew you were so respectful."

"Well," Bob replied. "It's the least I can do. We were married for twenty three years."

11

Familiar Faces

After Jesus had been crucified and had risen to the pearly gates, he spent much of his time there, meeting people as they arrived and offering the official heavenly greetings. One day he was standing there when this one particular gentleman arrived who looked terribly familiar.

"Excuse me, sir," Jesus inquired, "but you look very familiar to me. Do you mind if I ask what you did down on Earth?"

"Why no, young man," the elder replied. "I was a carpenter."

"A carpenter," Jesus thought to himself, "this is familiar, perhaps this could be my Earthly father!" So he continued out loud, "Sir, might I ask, did you have any children while on Earth?"

"Yes, I did," the old man affirmed. "I had a son, but he was taken from me."

Jesus thought, "Surely, this is Joseph!"

"Dad!" he shouted with much glee.

"Pinnochio?" the old man asked.

<u>12</u>

Geography

Where is Timbuktu?

Right between Timbuk-one and Timbuk-three.

13

Getting Older

I've been concerned about my aging lately. My wife, Cindy, has been giving me a hard time about all the gray hairs that I've been getting lately. But you know, she's a couple of years older than I am. I figure that as we age, she will experience those negative effects first and that will give me some time to adjust to them.

The other day, I was in the living room and Cindy was in the kitchen. I came across something in the newspaper that I thought she would be interested in so I called out to her, "Cindy!" There was no answer.

Right away, what did I think? Ah, ha! She's getting hard of hearing, first sign of aging and senility!

So I called out a second time, "Cindy!" Still no

answer. So I called out a third time, even louder, "CINDY!" And there was still no answer!

I was frustrated now. I got up and walked into the kitchen and asked her, "Cindy, haven't you heard me calling you?"

"Yes," she said, "I've answered you three times!"

14

Huh?

An elderly couple began to notice that they were forgetting things. They decided to take a memory course. A few weeks later they were visited by some old friends. The elderly gentleman was raving about the benefits of this course and how it had changed his and his wife's lives for the better.

His old friend was impressed. "What was the name of this memory course?" his friend asked.

The old man hesitated. "Let me think," he sighed. "It's a long stemmed flower, thorns on the stem, let's see, thorns, flower..."

"A rose?" his friend offered.

"Yes! That's it Rose! Rose," he called to his wife, "what's the name of that memory course we took?"

15

In The Beginning

There were three professionals who were arguing which of their professions was the most God-like. They were a surgeon, an architect and a politician.

The surgeon said, "God took a rib from Adam and created Eve. That is the skill of a surgeon."

The architect replied, "Yes, but God created order from chaos. Now that takes the mind of an architect."

Then the politician chipped in, "Yes, but who do you think created the chaos!?"

16

King Benny

One day a man named Benny was walking along the beach. He found a beautiful antique brass lamp that had washed up on the shore. He picked up the lamp and took it home with him. He took some cleanser and started to clean it up when a genie popped out of the lamp with a puff of magic smoke.

The genie said, "I am the captive of the lamp. You have released me. It is within my power to grant you every wish that you might have."

"Every wish?" the man asked.

"Every wish." the genie replied.

The man was very excited about the possibilities, but was not so far taken in that he didn't expect there to be some sort of catch.

"What's the catch?" he asked.

"There is but one condition," the genie responded. "You must never cut your hair."

"What happens if I cut my hair?" Benny asked.

The genie answered back, "If you cut your hair you will immediately be turned into a Grecian urn."

"That doesn't sound fun." Benny replied. "But having long hair is not too big a price to pay for having every wish granted."

He agreed and immediately wished for a million dollars. His wish was granted. He wished for a castle, for a court, a throne and many spectacular things. All his wishes were granted. Benny became famous throughout the land.

Many years went by, his hair grew and grew. It became very long and very heavy. It was driving Benny crazy.

One day, after many, many years, he came running through the court, his hair was trailing many feet behind him.

Benny started screaming at the top of his lungs, "I can't take it any more! This hair is driving me crazy! It's too heavy! It's too long! Call the royal barber! I don't care if I am turned into an urn!"

The barber was summoned and he came to Benny's side quickly.

"Shave it off!" Benny ordered. "Shave it all off!"

The barber did as he was told. He shaved Benny's head and Benny immediately was turned into a Grecian urn.

The moral: A Benny shaved is a Benny urned.

17

Late One Night

Late one night, I was out for a walk when I saw my friend Dave wandering around. He looked a little disoriented and as I approached him I saw that he had a big bump on his head. He had been bleeding, too.

"Dave," I queried, "are you OK?"

"No," he said, "my wife just hit me with her iron skillet!"

"Your wife? I thought she was visiting her mother this weekend," I said.

"So did I," he replied.

18

Leather

Have you noticed that those animal rights activists are more apt to be upset about fur over leather. It's because it's easier to harass rich women than motorcycle gangs.

19

More Money

There was this particular doctor who had done quite a lot of research in the area of cell reproduction and cloning. After some time he came to the realization that his private practice could double if he could clone himself.

After many attempts, he finally came up with a fully functioning reproduction of himself, and with some training this clone was able to practice medicine with an equal ability to the doctor.

Things went great! The doctor was beginning to double his income, making more and more every day!

Then, for no apparent reason, something went wrong. The clone began to be quite rude to the patients. He would treat them badly and often scream obscenities in the faces of the patients. The practice was beginning to drop off.

The doctor knew that he would have to do something or he would soon have no practice left. Word of this outrage was spreading quickly through the city.

He lured the clone to the tallest building in town. They went to the roof. The doctor pushed the clone from the roof and he fell to his death.

The doctor was arrested the next day.
The charges? Making an obscene clone fall.

20

My Uncle Mic

I'm of Irish heritage. My Uncle Mic just died recently, he was still back in the old country. I didn't get to attend the funeral but I heard it was quite a shebang! It seems that three days into the wake, the table that they had Mic's body spread out on, collapsed!

A couple of his friends were standing around wondering what to do. His old friend, Lesley, made a proposition. "If we raised up the head, we could slide a chair in beneath it. Then, with the head raised up, we could lift up the feet and slide a chair in under the feet. Then, with both ends raised up, we could raise up the middle and slide a third chair in underneath the middle! Do you think that would work?"

Mac said, "I believe it would!"

Lesley shouted out, "Can I get three chairs for Mic, please!"

The crowd shouted, "Hip, hip hurrah!"

21

Never Again

This gentleman went into the barbershop for a haircut. He was sitting in the chair and tried to strike up a little conversation with the man in the next chair.

"Have you been out fishing yet this spring," he asked.

"Nope," the man responded. "I tried fishing once. Didn't like it. Never tried it again."

"Well," the gentleman tried again. "How's your bowling, how's your average been?"

"I don't like bowling. I tried it once, never again," came the reply.

"Have you seen any good movies lately?" the gentleman tried once more.

"Nope, don't go to the movies," he answered. "Went once, didn't like it, never went back." As he answered, he noticed a red pickup pull up outside the shop. "Well, there's my boy to pick me up."

The gentleman responded, "I assume it's your only child?!"

22

OJ Justice

Knock. Knock.

Who's there?

O.J.

O.J. who?

O.K. You're on the jury!

23

Old Southern Comfort

A very, very old man was finally put into a home for the aged by his son. The family had thought it was best as he was now too old and just too feeble to care for himself.

The first day, he was sitting in the day room, he had only been there a short time, when the nurse looked over and saw him leaning horribly off to one side. Thinking that he would soon fall from his chair, she rushed over and sat the old man upright once more. Just a few short moments later, she looked over to check on him and he was leaning horribly over to the other side.

"Surely," she thought, "he's about to fall!"

She ran over to him and propped him up straight in his chair. He sat upright, straight and tall.

Sure enough, just moments later, he was leaning again, this time forward, just about to topple from his seat.

The nurse rushed back and propped him up once more. She called an orderly and requested a strap be brought. She took the strap and secured him upright into the chair. "This will do it," she thought. "He can't fall out now!"

That evening at dinner, the old man's family came to visit. "How are things going, dad?" the old man's son asked. "Are they treating you OK?"

"Well," the old man said after some hesitation, "they're not bad people. They just won't let me fart!"

24

One Liners

Don't take life too seriously, it isn't permanent.

• • •

"A man is incomplete until he is married. After that, he is finished."

• • •

A University is a fountain of knowledge at which all the students come to drink.

• • •

"I'm an excellent housekeeper. Every time I get a divorce, I keep the house."

Zsa Zsa Gabor

• • •

"A successful man is one who can make more money than his wife can spend. A successful woman is one who can find such a man."

Lana Turner

• • •

"Marriage is a great institution, but I'm not ready for an institution."

Mae West

• • •

"Marriage is bliss. Ignorance is bliss. Therefore....."

Unknown

• • •

"You're never completely worthless. You can always be used as a bad example."

Peggy Hancock

• • •

He who passes gas in church must sit in his own pew.

25

Performance Anxiety

The duffer stood over his tee shot for an eternity. He waggled, he looked up, looked down, waggled again, and never started his backswing.

Finally, exasperated, his partner shouted out to him, "What on earth is taking you so long?"

"My wife is up in the club house, watching me," the duffer replied.

"Good God, man," his companion cried out. "You'll never hit her from here!"

26

Rain, Sleet or Snow?

In a time not too long ago, a young Communist named Rudolf lived in New York City. Rudolf was married to a beautiful young woman named Olga. They lived together quite happily in the lower east side.

One wintery day in late November, Olga came in from her shopping, she placed her basket of groceries on the kitchen table and announced to Rudolf, "Rudolf, honey, it's sleeting out. I think it will turn to snow soon and by tomorrow, perhaps we can go sledding in the park."

Rudolf looked out the window. He studied the weather cautiously. He opened the window and stuck his hand out to feel the cold and the moisture. He closed the window and announced, "Olga, you silly thing, this is not sleet! It is only rain and just an ordinary rain at that, we shall have no snow, neither tonight nor tomorrow."

"Rudolf," Olga replied, "this is sleet! It is not rain, but sleet!"

Rudolf looked at Olga. He shook his head in disbelief and disappointment at her doubt in his meteorological knowledge. He then smiled and said, emphatically, "Olga, please! Rudolf, the Red, knows rain, dear!"

27

Richard

Richard's young son, age 5, came running into the living room from the garage. He was screaming, "Daddy, daddy, there's a lion in the garage!"

"Nonsense, son," Richard replied. "You know there isn't any lion out there. Come on, I'll show you."

Richard would have been 38 next month.

28

Shorts

A man went to see his doctor. "Doctor, doctor, I think I'm a kleptomaniac." "Don't worry," the doctor said, "I think you can take something for that."

• • •

What did one tonsil say to the other?
You better get dressed, the doctor is taking us out tonight.

• • •

What does it mean when a doctor says, "We caught this just in time"?
If you had waited any longer, it would have cleared up by itself.

• • •

What did the doctor say about your insomnia?
He said, I should drink a warm glass of milk after a hot bath.

Does it work?
I don't know. I can never finish drinking the bath.

• • •

Did you see any other doctors about this condition?
Yes, I did. One before you.
What quackery did he tell you?
He told me to come here.

• • •

Do you know why Jesus was born in a manger?
Mary was on an HMO.

• • •

How can you tell if someone is a kindergarten teacher?
You can tell by her tiny pupils.

• • •

Did you hear about the cross-eyed teacher that was fired from her job last week?
I understand that she couldn't control her pupils.

• • •

What do you call an unemployed jester?
Nobody's fool.

• • •

Did you hear about the two ships that collided on the high seas? One ship was carrying blue paint and the other was carrying purple paint. All the sailors were left marooned.

• • •

How about the ship that was carrying a cargo of yo-yo's from Taiwan. It sank 42 times.

• • •

Why do deep sea divers fall out of the boat backwards?
Because if they fell forward, they would be back in the boat.

• • •

I'm tired of hearing all this talk about how cats don't know how we feel. They do know how we feel. It's just that they don't care.

• • •

What do you call a fly with no wings?
A walk.

• • •

What's green and sings and is seen throughout the United States in Wal-marts?
Elvis Parsley.

• • •

Does it take longer in baseball to run from first base to second base, or does it take longer to run from second base to third base?
It takes longer to run from second base to third base because there is a short stop in between.

• • •

You know it's really cold outside...
when you see a dog frozen to the fire hydrant.

Ken Harmon

• • •

You know it's really windy outside...
when a hen lays the same egg three times.

Ken Harmon

• • •

How many home owners does it take to change a light bulb?
Only one, but it takes two weekends and seven trips to the hardware store.

• • •

How many psychiatrists does it take to change a light bulb?
One, but it takes ten years and the bulb has to really want to change.

• • •

How many Californians does it take to change a light bulb?

Fifteen, one to change the bulb and fourteen to share the experience.

• • •

How many male chauvinists does it take to change a light bulb?

None. Let her cook in the dark!

• • •

How many divorced males does it take to change a light bulb?

None, all the fixtures went with the house.

• • •

How many narcissists does it take to change a light bulb?

Only one. He holds it up while the world revolves around him to screw it in.

• • •

How many blondes does it take to change a light bulb?

Only one, if she can figure it out.

• • •

How many jugglers does it take to change a light bulb?

Two. One to screw it in and the other one to say, "I can do that!"

• • •

Who was the last person to box Joe Lewis?
The undertaker.

• • •

What's yellow and sleeps six?
A city maintenance truck!

• • •

Inside every thin man is a fat man trying to get out!   Lance Halve

29

Sixteen

Sixteen year old Jason asked his father for a car. "Dad," he asked. "I've turned sixteen now and I was wondering if you might buy me a car."

The father said, "Son, I will make a deal with you. You bring your grades up, go to church and cut your hair, then we'll talk about getting you a car."

Three months later the boy came back and said, "Dad, I've studied real hard and I've brought up my grades. I've been going to church each Sunday, I haven't missed a one. What about that car?"

"Jason, you still haven't cut your hair."

"Dad, I've been reading in the Bible and Jesus had long hair."

"Boy, keep reading, and you'll see that Jesus walked everywhere he went."

<u>30</u>

String 'Em Along

Three strings went into a bar for a drink. The bartender came over and glowered over them. "What do you want?!" he barked.

The first string said, "I would like a drink, please."

The bartender answered, "Get out, we don't serve your kind!" He looked at the second string, "What do you want!"

"I would like a drink, please"

"Didn't you hear me tell your friend! We don't want your kind in here!"

The third string quietly slipped off his stool and made his way into the bathroom. He closed and locked the door. Then he slipped himself into a strange configuration and shook himself until small fibers were hanging from his entire body. He opened the bathroom door and he went back to his stool. Upon seating himself, he called the bartender over and asked for a drink.

The bartender looked down at him and spoke gruffly, "Hey, aren't you one of those strings?!"

The string calmly answered, "Frayed knot."

31

T.V. and Ice Cream

An elderly husband and wife noticed that they were beginning to forget things. They were a little concerned about it so when they saw their physician next they told him of their worries.

The doctor told them that it was nothing to be concerned about. Many people their age began to forget small things and that many people found it helpful to write small notes to themselves to help them remember. The couple felt much better and left the doctor's office eager to try out their new system.

That evening, they sat in the living room watching some TV. "Dear," the wife asked, "will you please go out to the kitchen and fix me a bowl of ice cream?"

"Certainly," he replied.

"Perhaps you should write that down so you don't forget," she offered.

"Nonsense," he said, "I can remember a bowl of ice cream!"

"Well, I would like some strawberries on top, too, do you need to write it down?" she added.

"Of course not!" he assured, "I can remember a bowl of ice cream with strawberries!"

"OK, dear, but would you please put a little whipped cream on top? Do you need to write this down?" the wife asked.

"Don't be silly!" he cried. "My memory's not that bad. No problem. A bowl of ice cream with strawberries and whipped cream! I can remember that!"

With that, the husband left the living room and headed on into the kitchen. A few moments later, the wife heard a great commotion of pots and pans. Fifteen minutes later, the husband returned and handed the wife a plate of bacon and eggs.

She looked down at the plate, a slight frown appeared on her face. She looked back up to her husband and asked, "Hey, where's the toast?"

32

Texas Divorce

What does an Oklahoma twister and a Texas divorce have in common?

Anyway you look at it, some old boy is going to lose his trailer.

33

The 3 Cannibals

Did you hear about that little cannibal boy that got kicked out of school last week?

He got caught buttering up the teacher.

• • •

Why don't cannibals eat clowns?

They taste funny.

• • •

Did you hear about the cannibal that passed his brother in the woods?

He did.

34

The Bad Swing

This one particular duffer had a miserable game one day. He felt so badly that he skipped the clubhouse and decided to head straight home. As he was heading to his car in the parking lot, he noticed just outside the lot a police car with the lights flashing. As he neared his car, an officer stepped out of the patrol car and hurried up to the melancholy golfer.

"Excuse me," the officer started, "but did you tee off from the sixteenth hole about twenty minutes ago?"

"Why yes, I did," the weekend warrior replied.

"Did you happen to hook your ball, so that it went over the trees and off the course?" the trooper queried.

"Yes, it was a poor shot, but how did you know?" the club member asked.

"Well," said the policeman very seriously, "your ball flew out onto the highway and crashed through a windshield. The car went out of control, running five other vehicles off the road and causing a fire truck to crash. That fire truck was on its way to a fire, and so that building is a complete and total loss. I want to know what you are going to do about this?"

"Hmmm," the golfer mused. "I think I need to close my stance, keep my head down and tighten my grip."

<u>35</u>

The Bank Loan

The frog had lived in the same pond on the same lily pad for many a year now. He was happy with his pond and his lily pad was quite comfortable, but he thought it might be time for a change. He didn't want to move so he thought the answer might be to remodel his comfortable lily pad."

The frog hopped down to his local Savings and Loan. He hopped up to a teller and said, "Excuse me, please, but I would like to take out a loan to remodel my lily pad."

The teller looked down over her counter and said, "You'll have to go to the loan department and see Ms. Paddywack. She's the loan officer.

So the frog hopped over to the loan department and asked for Ms. Paddywack. Soon he stood before a matronly lady who towered over the little green guy.

"Yes?" she asked.

"I would like to remodel my lily pad," the frog explained. "I need a loan, please."

"Do you have any collateral?" Ms. Paddywack asked.

"Collateral? What's collateral?" the frog asked, perplexed.

Ms. Paddywack explained, "Collateral is something of value that we can take in case you default on your loan."

"Oh," the frog said. He reached into his pocket and pulled out a small item. "All I have is this." The frog handed the object to Ms. Paddywack.

Ms. Paddywack stared down into her hand at the small strange object and said to the frog, "Hold on, just a minute, Mr. Frog. I will need to ask my supervisor about this."

Ms. Paddywack walked down the hall to the supervisor's office and explained, "The frog wants a loan and all he has for collateral is this, and I don't even know what this is!"

The supervisor looked in her hand, shook his head and said, "It's a knick-knack, Paddywack, give the frog a loan!"

36

The Bear

These two fellows went backpacking together. When they pulled up to the trail head the fellows got out their gear. The one pulled out his heavy hiking boots with their Vibram soles and two pair of socks and meticulously began to prepare his feet for the day's march. The other pulled out a thin pair of cotton footies and some Nike racing flats.

"What are you doing? Are you planning on hiking in those running shoes?" the experienced hiker asked.

"Yep, it's in case we see a bear," the novice explained.

"You can't out run a bear!" the hiker argued.

The new hiker reasoned, "I don't have to outrun the bear, all I have to do is out run you!"

37

The Bet

A computer programmer and an engineer were sitting next to one another on an airplane. The programmer leaned over and asked the engineer if he wanted to play a fun game. The engineer replied that he wanted to get some sleep, "No thank you."

The programmer persisted. "Listen," he said, "it's a real easy game. I ask you a question and, if you don't know the answer, you pay me $5. Then you ask me a question, and if I don't know, I pay you $5."

The engineer replied that he just wanted to get some sleep and he again refused.

The programmer, for some reason, really wanted to play and now a little agitated and excited he persisted, "Ok," he said, "I'll tell you what, if you don't know, you pay me $5, and if I don't know, I'll pay you $50!"

This got the engineer's attention, so he agreed to the game. The programmer asked the first question, "What is the distance from the Earth to the moon?" The engineer didn't say a word, he reached into his wallet and gave the programmer $5.

Next, the engineer asked the programmer, "What goes up a hill with three legs and comes down on four?" The programmer looked puzzled, he took out his laptop and began to utilize his references. The engineer turned away and closed his eyes. After about an hour, the programmer woke up the engineer and handed him $50. The engineer took it and returned to sleep.

The programmer was still puzzled and very curious, so after a few moments, he asked the engineer, "Well, what is it?" The engineer didn't say a word. He reached into his wallet, handed the programmer $5, turned away and went back to sleep.

38

The Blacksmith

A blacksmith was working a horseshoe into shape. He would put the iron into the fire until it was red hot, then he would pull it out and with his tongs, holding it in place on the anvil, the blacksmith would hammer away. As he finished the shaped shoe, he tossed it into the dirt in front of him.

An old sun crazed cow poke came walking by just a few moments later. He spied the cooling shoe in the dirt and reached down to pick it up. As he realized the shoe was still intensely hot by the burning and searing of his carpal flesh, he tossed the shoe back into the dirt.

"Mighty hot?!" stated the blacksmith.

"Nope," denied the surprised wrangler, "it just don't take me long to look at a horseshoe!"

39

The Bobbits

I heard that the Bobbits have gotten back together. Yes. They really are trying to make a fresh start. In fact, they're going to church together and both have even started teaching Sunday school. He's teaching Second Peter and she's teaching Acts!

40

The Cannon

There was a small community that had a Civil War cannon on display in the town square's center. All the people of the town were very proud of their little piece of history and they hired a man just to clean and shine the cannon daily.

Each day he would report to work. He would then wash the cannon very cautiously and deliberately. It took him all morning long. Then he would break for lunch. After lunch, he would shine and buff the cannon. It sparkled and shined.

Each year on his annual evaluation. The man was asked if he enjoyed his job. "Oh, yes!" the cannon cleaner would say. "I get to work outside. There's not much stress. I enjoy it very much."

Many years passed.

One day the cannon cleaner came in to work and said that he was leaving.

"Why?" the city manager asked. "I thought you liked your work."

"I do," he answered. "I love it. The fact is, each pay check, I've put a little back. Over the years, I've socked quite a bit away. Truth is, I've bought my own cannon, and now, I'm going into business for myself!"

41

The Casket

A funeral procession was making it's way up a long hill in San Francisco when the hearse hit a rather hefty hole. The back door came undone and the casket slid right out of the back, onto the street and began to pick up speed rapidly as it slid down the hill. The casket went through several intersections, just barely making it's way through traffic. Through each intersection, pedestrians and vehicles had to swerve and dodge in order to avoid the speeding casket as it careened faster and faster toward the bottom of the hill.

At the bottom, this long steep boulevard came to an abrupt end as it merged with a perpendicular byway. The casket slid across this final intersection and slammed into the curb. As it hit this great bump, the casket latch broke and the cover flew ajar. The casket continued through a plate glass door into a drug store crashing into the pharmacist's counter. As it finally came to rest, the lid flew open and the corpse inside bolted upright.

Behind the counter stood an elderly and rather near-sighted gentleman. The white haired pharmacist peered across the counter into the face of the body. "May I help you?" he asked.

The body replied, "Yeah, do you have anything to stop this dang coffin?"

42

The Church Goer

The silver haired gentleman came home from church sporting a black eye. His wife asked him what happened. She had broken her leg that week and so had stayed at home.

"Well," the old fellow explained, "we were all getting ready to sing hymns. The reverend had us all stand up and when we stood, I noticed that the woman in the pew in front of me had her dress all tucked up between her cheeks. Well, I thought that this would be mighty embarrassing if she knew it, so I reached forward and pulled the material out. I don't know what she thought I was doing, but she turned around and slapped me in the eye!"

The next week came and the wife, still feeling poorly, chose to stay home again. "Mind your manners," she warned as her husband left the house.

Sure enough, a couple of hours later, he returned with his other eye a brighter shade of the bruise from last week! "What happened now?" his wife questioned.

"Well, we were getting ready to sing hymns and we all stood up. That same lady was right in front of me. Well, she got up and sure enough she had her skirt tucked in between her cheeks. The fellow beside me reached forward and pulled it out. I knew she didn't like that so I reached ahead and tucked it back in."

43

The City Crew

The street maintenance crew drove out to their work site. After a few minutes one of the guys came up to the foreman.

"I've got some bad news for you, boss," he said. "We forgot to pick up our shovels."

"That's OK, I'll go get them," the foreman replied. "Just lean on one another until I get back."

44

The Dead Dog

A woman came home from work one day to find her beloved dog lying completely still. She called for him and he continued to lay there. She went over to him and shook him. No response.

She quickly grabbed up the beast and hurried to her car. She drove lickety split to her veterinarian's office.

"I came home and found my dog like this!" she cried.

A brief examination and the vet pronounced the dog dead.

"Are you sure," the woman pleaded, "he's been such a great pet. I really hate to see him go. Is there nothing else that can be done?"

"There is one more thing we can try," the vet answered.

He went to the back and brought in a small kitten. He held the kitten up to the dog's nose. He then circled the dog's head with the small feline. After which he moved the kitten up and down from the head to tail many times.

"That confirms it," the doctor insisted. "The dog is dead."

"Oh dear," the woman sighed. "I really was afraid of that. How much do I owe you?"

The vet answered, "That will be $3030.00."

"What!" the pet lover screamed. "$3030.00, what for?"

"It's $30 for the office visit, and $3000 for the cat scan, of course!"

45

The Diamond Ring

A man was sitting next to an empty seat in an airplane when a beautiful young woman came down the aisle and seated herself next to him. The man noticed that she had on her finger the biggest diamond that he had ever seen. He couldn't help but stare. Finally, he could contain himself no longer and remarked to the young lady how exquisite her diamond was.

She thanked him very much, and added, "Yes, it is one of the most beautiful and flawless diamonds in the world, it's a Johnston diamond, but unfortunately, it has a terrible curse associated with it."

"Really," the man was intrigued, "What might that curse be?"

"Mr. Johnston," she replied.

46

The Dog

The Adams family got a new dog. It was a cute dog, but not very house broken. The second week, the mutt chewed a hole in the middle of the living room carpet. Old man Adams began to scream, "That's it. I'm getting rid of that dog tonight!"

"Please, no!" cried little Danny. "I'll train him, I promise."

"It seems a little too late for that," his father snapped.

"No, it's not, I'll teach him to lie on the hole and not move!"

47

The Drunk

This old alcoholic was at his wit's end one cold December night. The weather was terrible, ice and snow had fallen all day. He needed to get to the liquor store before it closed. He finally scrounged up enough cash for a pint, and out he went.

Three blocks away, he made his purchase, put the bottle into his back pocket and hurried back toward his flat. Just as he reached his building's front stair stoop, he slipped and came crashing down. As he lay on the icy sidewalk, he began to feel a warm liquid flowing through his pants.

"I sure hope that's blood," he thought.

48

The Eagle Kill

A game warden was making his rounds when he suddenly heard the blast of several gun shots. It was not hunting season and with great concern he began to make his way to the direction of the blasts. As he approached, he continued to hear periodic gunshots. He drew his own gun and made his way cautiously.

He peered through some bushes and brush and there he spotted a small camp. A ragged tent was set up, an old beat-up pickup truck sat off to the side, three dirty faced children were playing with some sticks behind the truck. A man with an old rifle stood to the left of a woman that was seated in front of a small fire plucking feathers from ...a bald eagle! Then he noticed two more of the majestic birds!

Good God! The officer was outraged. It was a bald eagle! They had been hunting bald eagles!

He went forward, "Put your hands into the air!" he cried. "You are under arrest for the killing of a protected species."

The man looked down, and then back up at the ranger. "Please," he said, "my family is starving. I've been out of work for five months, I haven't been able to find work anywhere, we're now homeless and everything that you see here is the total amount of our possessions. We're broke and have nothing. I only hunted these birds because my wife and my children are starving. I couldn't find any other game! Please don't arrest me!" he pleaded.

The ranger looked at the man, his wife dressed in rags and the dirty and scruffy children that had run to the feet of the poor woman. His heart melted.

After many moments, he holstered his revolver. "OK," he said, "but you need to pack things up and move on." Then he added, "You know, I'm curious. What does a bald eagle taste like?"

The man answered, "Oh, it's kind of a cross between the spotted owl and the whooping crane."

49

The Explorers

Two boys were off exploring some fields neighboring their community. They had walked far and were covering territory that neither had seen before. As they crossed this one particular field, they noticed some pile of rock that had obviously been stacked years before, the pile had been circular, but through the many years, many of the rock and fallen off to the side and created a look of noticeable abandonment.

The boys came to the edge of the wall and noticed that this structure used to form the wall of a well as the rock surrounded a deep, deep hole. The boys peered down into the darkness trying to see if there was still water present.

They could see nothing. One of the boys picked up a small rock and dropped it into the darkness of the hole. They leaned forward and listened intently. Nothing. All they heard was the sound of birds chirping from the nearby trees and the rustle of the tall grass in the warm summer breeze. "This hole must really be deep!" they thought.

The second boy picked up a much larger rock and with some difficulty managed to drop it into the darkness of the chasm. They listened, ears turned to the darkness, waiting for some indication of the bottom. Still nothing.

The boys spotted a length of utility pole over on the north end of the field. They thought surely this pole will make some noise. They struggled and grunted and groaned and were finally able to get the pole to the edge of the well. They labored intently and eventually managed to drop the pole into the deep, dark hole. They listened and listened and heard nothing.

Then, suddenly, the strangest thing happened. From across the field, came running a goat. The little goat came faster and faster directly toward them as they leaned over the well. As they saw the goat rapidly approaching they leaped back from the edge of the wall. As they jumped back, the little goat sprang forward, over the well wall and down into the deep darkness.

They stood puzzled. Wondering what on Earth happened. Where did the goat come from? Why did he leap into the well? What's going on here?

As they stood there dumbfounded, a farmer approached. He asked, "Boys, did either of you happen to see a goat around here?"

The boys described the unusual event of moments before. "Yes, this goat just came running up to us as fast as he could and then he jumped over this wall and down into this hole!"

The farmer stood quietly for a moment, and then said, "That couldn't have been my goat. My goat was tied up to a utility pole."

50

The First Flight

This little fellow was taking his first plane ride, ever, on a trip from Cleveland to Dallas. He was very nervous and did not feel well about it at all. His boarding pass seated him next to the window. He was looking out the window fretting about the upcoming flight, when this guy sat down next to the worried passenger. This guy was some huge cowboy from Texas.

The jet took off, and the Texan quickly fell asleep, oblivious to everything around him, and began to snore quite loudly. The small frightened passenger began to feel quite ill. He was airsick. He started to sweat and felt nauseous. He was too timid and fearful to wake the giant man next to him. Before long, sure enough, the meek fellow vomited right into the lap of the rough and tumble Texan. The little guy was horrified and immediately began to worry about what to do when the Texan would wake up.

The cowboy finally awakened and looked down, and saw the nasty mess that covered his lap. He looked over at the frightened little man and frowned. The little man suggested, "I hope you are feeling a little better now!"

51

The First Watch

Alexander the Great was one of the first generals to recognize the need for the coordinated movement of troops. His area of conquest was vast and his troops were stationed throughout the known world of his time. He knew that in order to keep his rule intact, a universal method of time keeping would be necessary.

He went to his wise men and explained the problem. The wise men told him that what would be necessary would be to develop some type of transportable devices that could maintain a consistent synchronized method telling time. These devices, they added, could be sent among his generals throughout the vast regions and each general would be aware of an accurate time that could be used in coordinating troop movements and enemy attacks.

Alexander went to his magician and explained the problem and the suggestions of the wise men. The magician opened his books of magic and after some time reported to the general that he had the solution. Alexander was elated and beckoned the magician to his chambers immediately.

The magician arrived and waltzed into the room with the air of a peacock, he was so proud of his discovery. He held up a small strip of cloth. This cloth could be tied about the wrist of the individual and after certain increments of time, the cloth would change colors. The magician confided that this was possible by dipping the cloth in a certain sequence of chemicals that would not harm the person wearing the swatch. The cloth would consistently turn colors every other hour. This could thus be worn by the generals and provide a synchronized method of telling time no matter where they were in Alexander's great domain.

This marvelous invention came to be known as "Alexander's Rag Time Band"!

52

The Glass Eye

There was this man who had one glass eye. He also owned a motorcycle and would like to drive it very, very fast. All of his friends would caution him, that he shouldn't go so fast. That one day he would have a terrible accident. He should slow down. The man would just laugh. He had no fear.

One day, he was in a terrible wreck. He was driving very rapidly down a lonely deserted stretch of country road. He went around this one blind corner and there on the other side of the turn was a BMW with two ophthalmologists. They were driving in the center of the road, just as was the motorcyclist. The cyclist swerved, just barely avoiding the car. However, he lost control of the bike and veered off the road into a ditch and hit his head. He was unconscious.

The doctors were horrified! They leapt from the car and examined the cyclist. They determined that outside of some severe eye damage, the man would be OK. They decided to take the man into their clinic and they proceeded to fix the eye the best way they knew how. Then, fearing the publicity of their accident, they decided to take the man back out to the road side and drop him off.

The next day the doctors saw this headline: Mysterious accident involving cyclist with two glass eyes!

53

The Guillotine

It was during the tremendous turmoil of the French revolution. This one particular day, three gentlemen were being led to their executions, a priest, a common drunkard and an engineer.

The priest was the first to be led over to the guillotine. As they began to lie him down, he made a request. "Please," he cried, "let me lie face up. I wish to look up to the heavens and to my God in my last moments."

The executioners agreed. They put him face up and the priest began to pray fervently. They released the blade and as it came crashing down, it suddenly and miraculously stopped just inches away from the priest's neck. The executioners interpreted this as divine intervention and released the priest. He hurriedly left, praising God.

The drunk was next. What had happened to the priest did not go unnoticed with him, so he, too, requested that he be placed face up and as they put him there, he, too, started to pray like he had never prayed before!

The blade was released and it halted just inches away from the drunkard's neck. The executioners released him and he rushed away praising God.

Finally, the engineer was led up the steps. Not wanting to do things differently, the engineer requested to be placed face up. The executioners obeyed the request and just moments before they released the giant blade, the engineer shouted out, "Hold on, I think I see your problem."

54

The Interview

The manager was doing the interviews for the new waitress position down at Joe's Diner. He was interviewing Mary Lou.

"I see your birthday is July 17th. What year?" he asked.

"Every year," Mary Lou answered.

55

The Little Girl

A little girl went running into the living room and asked her mother, "Mommy, mommy the boys are outside playing, can I go out and play with them?"

"No," her mother replied, "those boys are too rough."

"Can I play if I find some smooth ones?"

56

The Mean Dog

There was once a fellow who lived on the South side of Chicago. He had this tremendous Doberman pinscher. The dog was viscous. He claimed that it was the meanest dog in the world. Every day he would end up in this one particular bar. He would tie the dog to a parking meter outside. He would brag about how mean his dog was. It would snarl and snap at people passing by and he would laugh at them as they jumped.

One night, late into the evening, a gentleman came into the bar inquiring, "Does anyone in here own the Doberman pinscher outside?"

"I do," the man snapped. "And I'll have you know, that is the meanest darn dog in the world!"

"Yeah?" asked the newcomer.

"Darn right!" the dog owner barked back.

"Well," the gentleman responded, "my dog just killed it."

"What!?" the dog owner exclaimed, his chin dropped to the counter. "How could that be? My dog is the meanest dog in the world! What kind of dog do you have?"

"I own a poodle." the man answered softly.

"A poodle!" The dog owner was astounded. "How could your poodle kill my dog? How could your poodle kill my Doberman?"

"She got caught in his throat." he answered.

57

The Mouse Trap

A man ran into the hardware store and shouted at the clerk, "Hey there, I need a mouse trap, and hurry, I have to catch a bus!"

"I'm sorry," the salesman replied. "We don't have any that big."

58

The Penguins

This good old boy was driving his pickup truck down the highway one morning, when he saw this delivery truck with a broken axle along side of the road.

The old boy, being a helpful and friendly fellow, stopped and asked the delivery driver what he could do to help.

"Well," the driver said, "I've got this here load of penguins in the back of my truck and I'm supposed to have them to the zoo by noon. If we could load all them crates into the back of your pickup, do you think you could take them to the zoo for me?"

"Sure," the old boy replied, "I would be happy to do it!"

So the two of them worked fast and hard moving all of the crates of penguins from the back of the delivery truck into the back of the pickup truck. The old boy headed to the zoo while the delivery man stayed and waited for the tow truck.

The next day, the delivery driver was out and about in another part of town, when, lo and behold, he spied that old boy driving down the street in his pickup and would you believe it, he had his cab plumb full of those penguins!

The delvery driver began to chase after the old boy, honking his horn and trying to wave him down. After some time, he finallly caught up to the pickup truck. The delivery driver jumped from his truck and ran to the pickup, screaming, "What are you doing? What are you doing? What on Earth are you doing? I thought I told you to take those penguins to the zoo!"

"I did," replied the old boy. "We had such a dang good time, that today, I'm taking them to the movies!"

59

The Pirate

A tourist went into a sea side bar. Up at the counter was a grizzled and weather beaten old man, dressed in the traditional garb of an old sailor. The poor man had seen his days, obviously, he had a patch over his left eye, a steel hook for a right hand and a wooden peg attached at the left knee.

The tourist sat down a few stools over from the old mariner and watched as the seafarer mournfully swallowed the last bit of ale in his glass.

"Would you like to have another, on me?" the visitor asked.

"Certainly, I would" the codger replied. "I would be happy to repay ye with stories from me younger days."

"I would like to hear how you lost your leg," the landlubber suggested as the bartender brought them both a round.

"Well," the sailor replied, "T'isn't a great story, a shark bit it off one day down in the Caribbean. Solid mahoganies the replacement, a beautiful piece of wood, aye, and fine craftsmanship, too."

"How about that hook? How did you lose your hand?"

"Lost 'er in a sword fight. Dang near lost me life, I did. The fellow wacked it off with'n a clean sweep, I was scramblin' to try to get a holt of me blade with me other hand, and the bloody bloke was runnin' up to me to whack me in the neck, he was. Luckily fer me, one of me mates was standing near and he shot the bugger in the head with'n his pistol, he did. The fellow dropped to me feet. It was close! But it's stainless steel it is, and fine craftsmanship!"

"How did you lose your eye?"

"Well, it was a windy day. I had to climb up the

main mast to take look out fer a bit. The day was surly and it looked like a storm was to break out in just about a bit. As I got to the top of the main mast and was to climb on into the crow's nest fer me turn at look out, I heard the call of a 'ungry and angry seagull. I heard that bird's call and looked up and as I did the bird let one rip and the poop dropped right into me eye!"

"But how did that cause you to lose your eye?" the visitor inquired.

"It was me first day to 'ave me hook!"

60

The Preacher

This Baptist minister was walking down the street admiring the day when he spied across the way a small child jumping up trying to press the doorbell of the house on who's porch he was standing. "That young boy looks as though he could use some help," the young minister thought to himself. Seeing it as an opportunity to serve, the young man of God crossed the street and headed up to the porch. "Do you need some help there, young man?" he asked the small boy. "Mister," the boy replied, "could you ring the doorbell?" "Why certainly," the minister replied. He then reached out easily and pressed the button that the tiny lad had so earnestly been trying to reach. They heard the bell ring inside the house. The young boy exclaimed, "OK, mister, now run like heck!"

61

The Psychiatrist

A man went to the psychiatrist. "What seems to be the trouble?" the doctor asked.

"Well, I have this terrible inferiority complex." the man answered. "I'm hoping you can help me."

"Please, sit down, let me ask you some questions," the doctor replied.

The doctor interviewed the gentleman for some time. After an hour had lapsed, the doctor announced, "I have great news for you! You don't have an inferiority complex. You are inferior!"

62

The Refrigerator Rabbit

Mrs. McGregor was greatly surprised the other morning. She wakened in the middle of the night and could not get back to sleep. After lying quietly in bed for some time, she decided that she would go to the kitchen and fix herself a warm glass of milk. "That would do the trick, she thought." So she got up out of bed, walked into the kitchen and opened the refrigerator door. There to her astonishment sat a rather large brown and white rabbit!

"What are you doing in there!" she shrieked.

"Well," said the rabbit, "this is a Westinghouse refrigerator, isn't it?"

"Yes," Mrs. McGregor replied.

"I'm westing," explained the rabbit.

63

The Rescue

This table of seven women were having lunch together at the local steak place. They get together once a month to celebrate, oh, birthdays or anniversaries or, well, anything that might give them an excuse to celebrate. They just enjoyed getting together. Of course, they looked forward to it each month with much excitement and anticipation. It was great fun.

Anyway, this one particular day they were all together. Martha was in a particularly good mood, she was laughing and carrying on and was already on her third glass of wine. I could tell she was an accident waiting to happen. She was cutting her meat into too large of bites, she wasn't chewing it well at all and was constantly talking and laughing while eating! Sure enough, at one point, someone cracked a great joke while Martha was chewing on this big piece of sirloin.

She laughed and suddenly inhaled that chunk of steak right into her windpipe! She couldn't breathe, she couldn't talk, her hands went up into the international choking signal. She panicked. She jumped up from her chair and started to run about the room, her hands clutching to her throat, she was quickly turning blue. Everyone was horrified, no one knew what to do and sat frozen with fork poised in mid bite.

Suddenly, from a corner table a young hero jumped out of his seat and ran to the woman. "Quick! Lady! I know what to do!" he cried. "Bend over!"

Martha did what she was told. The do-gooder quickly raised Martha's skirt and placed his face between her two cheeks. That piece of meat shot out of her mouth with a popping noise. Martha began to breathe normally again. She turned to the young man and began to mutter, "Thank you, thank you!" over and over and over again. The rest of the place jumped to their feet into a standing ovation for the guy. He was a hero! He went back to his seat and sat down. His friend acknowledged his success, "That was great," he said. "What did you do?"

"Oh, it was nothing," our hero explained. "I learned it in first aide. It is the hind lick maneuver."

64

The Royal Potato

Once upon a time there was the first place grand prize winning Idaho Russet Potato. He married the most beautiful and wonderful grand prize winning Red Potato. They lived happily together in a terrific cottage in a very pleasant neighborhood. The time came when they had a small baby girl. They named her Sweet Potato.

Sweet Potato had a fantastic childhood. She was smart, articulate and friendly. She grew into a beautiful young adolescent spud. Her parents were proud of her.

Before her parents realized it, it was time for young Sweet Potato to head off to school. She chose a small college not to far from home.

Christmas break arrived and so did Sweet Potato. She came through the door with a stupendous level of excitement. She was bubbling over and could not sit still! "Mom, dad," she cried out with joy, "I'm engaged! I'm getting married!"

This was not what mom and dad had anticipated. They had many wonderful plans for their precocious young daughter, whose marriage should come much later.

"Hold on," daddy potato cried out. "Slow down," father continued, "We have not even met this young man. We don't even know who he is or what his name is!"

"He's absolutely wonderful," Sweet Potato assured her parents. "He has a steady job, it's great! He's on TV! He's a newsman. His name is Dan Rather!"

"Whoa!" father stated firmly. "This will not be allowed! Dan Rather? Why, he is just a common-tater!"

65

The Shopping Trip

Mrs. Davis walked up to the manager of the department store. "Excuse me," she asked, "but are you hiring any help?"

"No, madam," he said. "We already have the staff we need."

"Then would you mind getting some one to help me?" she asked.

66

The Siamese Twins

Why did the Siamese twins go to England?

It was the other one's turn to drive.

67

The Skeleton

A skeleton walked into a bar and said to the bartender, "Give me a beer and a mop."

68

The Talking Frog

An elderly man was hobbling his way down the street. He was taking his time, stopping frequently to rest and catch his breath. As he passed a particular alley, he began to hear high pitched shouts for help. He looked down the alley and could see no one. He made his way carefully into the alley, listening for the cries. He soon found a stack of boxes. He moved them to the side with his cane and there sat a big green frog.

"Help me," the frog cried. "I'm a very young and beautiful woman who has fallen prey to a terrible spell. If you only kiss me, I will turn back into a beautiful young woman. If only you will kiss me, I will be eternally grateful. I will return to your home with you. I will cook for you. I will clean your house and wash your laundry. I will massage your tired muscles and I will even share your bed with you."

The old man pondered for a moment, bent over and picked up the frog. He then slid the frog into the side pocket of his jacket. He turned around and began to leave the alley.

"Hey," the frog exclaimed. "Aren't you going to kiss me?"

"Believe me, at my age, a talking frog is much more interesting."

69

The Toe

The other day I was traveling down the expressway, trafface was heavy, and things seemed to be moving rather slowly.

In the distance, from behind, I began to make out the faint cry of a siren. As the vehicle came closer and the noise of the warning became louder, I began to notice vehicles pulling over as much as they could on the crowded and congested dispersal loop. I could tell the vehicle was an ambulance.

Everyone had moved to the right as best as they could and still the ambulance was having some trouble weaving in and out of the dense traffic.

Just as the emergency vehicle passed me, it swerved. Apparently, to miss some broken glass toward the shoulder of the asphalt. As it swerved, somehow, the back door flew open and an ice chest spilled onto the freeway. With the next swerve the door slammed shut once more.

I hopped out of my car and dashed over to the ice chest. It had opened slightly. I looked in, and, oh, God, it was a human toe! A severed human toe laying in a bed of ice.

I looked up and the ambulance was gone. So, I did the only thing I could do. I called a toe truck.

<u>70</u>

The Train Ride

A young couple was watching the beautiful scenery pass by from a train window. It was a wonderful relaxing ride. Then the train's whistle began to blast, and blast, and blast again! Each blast was longer and seemed louder than the blast before. Something must be wrong!

Suddenly, the train derailed, it seemed to leap from the tracks as it careened several hundred yards across very bumpy pasture land and then just as mysteriously came to rest once again on the tracks with a giant bump.

The young man said, "I'm going forward to the engineer and see what this commotion was all about!"

He worked his way through the forward cars and came finally to the engine compartment.

"What happened," he inquired.

"I saw this man on the tracks," said the engineer, "so I kept blowing and blowing the whistle, but he simply would not budge! I was afraid I was going to run him over!"

"Well, you should have run him over instead of endangering all of the lives on this train!" the young man insisted.

"That's exactly what I decided to do," the engineer replied. "But as soon as I got real close to him, he tried to run away!"

71

The Transplant

A secretary had been having some incredibly severe headaches for several months. She finally decided to see her physician. After the physician had run several tests, he referred her on to a specialist. The specialist ran more tests and after thousands of dollars worth, he called her in for a consultation.

"I have some rather troubling news for you," he said. "We have found that you are suffering from a very rare and lethal form of a brain disorder. It is very rapid and past cases have shown that the degeneration begins to occur non-stop from this point."

"Oh, my goodness!" she exclaimed. "You mean, I'm going to die?"

"Well," the specialist said, "there is one hope.

Recent surgical procedures have been tried, with a great deal of success in this type of problem."

"I would like to hear more," she said. "Please continue."

"The procedure is a brain transplant. I know it sounds incredible, and it is a very expensive procedure. But, we have seen tremendous positive results in recent cases. It's very hopeful."

"I have some excellent insurance with my company, please go on," she said.

"As I said, it is a very expensive procedure and should be done immediately," the doctor explained. "Right now, we do have three options to choose from, much like a heart transplant, the brain comes from a very recently deceased individual whose brain we have been able to ice and preserve."

"How much does it cost?" the secretary queried.

"That depends on which brain you choose," the doctor stated. "Your first choice comes from a marine biologist and the fee for that brain is $300,000."

The secretary said, "I believe my coverage would allow for that, what other options do I have?"

"Well," the specialist continued, "the next choice is a rocket scientist's brain. That one runs $600,000."

"A rocket scientist!" the secretary exclaimed. "I believe my coverage could still swing that. What's my third option?" she asked.

"Finally, we have the brain of a middle manager. That brain runs five million dollars."

The secretary was nearly speechless. "Goodness," she exclaimed, "why is that one so high!"

"Never been used."

72

The Turtle

A turtle was making his way home from the neighborhood pub very, very early one morning. He was only a couple of blocks from his house when he was attacked by three snails.

Later, he was being interviewed by the police. "Can you tell us what happened?" the officer in charged asked.

"Not really," the turtle replied. "It all happened so fast!"

73

The Unfaithful Wife

An unfaithful wife was hugging and kissing her lover in a hotel room when suddenly someone started banging on the door, shouting. "Oh my God," exclaimed the woman, "that's my husband, quick jump out the window!"

"I can't," replied the lover. "We're on the thirteenth floor!"

"For crying out loud," the woman cried, "this is no time to be superstitious!"

74

The Vagabond

A nineteenth century vagabond was roaming the English countryside. It was quite late and he was hungry and tired when he came to an inn, a large hand painted sign out front identified the stop as: George and the Dragon.

The tattered man knocked loudly on the door, as it was quite late and all the lights were turned out. He knocked again and again until finally an upper shutter flew open and a shrill voice called out to him, "What is it?"

"I was wondering," the old man asked, "could you spare some vittles?"

"No," shrieked the answer, "we have nothing for the likes of you!"

"Perhaps, you might have an extra bed?"

"No," she said. "We're full up."

"Do you suppose, I could use the privy?" he tried again.

"No! Now be gone with you!" came the shrewish call.

"Perhaps..." he tried once more.

"What is it now?!" she screamed.

"I was wondering if I might have a word with George?"

75

The Visit

A Baptist minister was making the rounds of his members one day when he knocked on the door of this one particular house. "Come in. Come in," he heard someone say. He opened the door and walked in, seeing no one he said in a loud voice, "Hello?" "Come in, come in," he again heard the calls. He proceeded down the hall. "Hello?" he asked expectantly. "Come in, come in." He opened a door and walked into the kitchen, where he was greeted by a ferocious looking and snarling German Shepherd. The dog leaped at the man and pinned him against the wall with his huge paws, barking and snarling at this man of God. The preacher, still perplexed, then noticed in the corner, a cage housing a green parrot. The parrot again said, "Come in, come in." The minister, now terrified, looked over at the parrot and said, "You stupid bird, don't you know anything else to say?!"

"Sic 'em." the bird replied.

76

The Wedding

At a wedding, a friend told me of this announcement on the back of the bulletin. Please do not throw rice or bird seed at the wedding couple. If you do, they will eat it and blow up.

77

The Young, The Good & The Legal

A cruise ship was tossed back and forth in a terrible storm. During the rough night, the ship went down and a handful of survivors were washed up on a small desert island without any food or water.

The next morning they could see the ship's wreckage located on a sand bar not too far from the shore. Unfortunately, the inlet between the shore and sand bar was filled with hungry sharks.

The strongest young man volunteered to swim out to the ship and bring back some food and water. "I'm strong and a good swimmer," he said. "I believe I can make it." He started out.

Sure enough, it wasn't long before the sharks attacked and the rest of the survivors watched, horrified, from the shore as the young man was torn and devoured.

Days past, the surviving passengers were not going to survive if they did not get some fresh water and food soon.

A clergy stood up and announced, "I've been praying for our safety and survival for days. Last night I had a dream, that I made it to the ship and returned with the food and water. I believe that I can make it! The Lord will protect me."

He started across the small barrier of shark ridden water. It wasn't long before he, too, was mutilated and devoured. The others' hopes were dashed.

The hungry survivors waited a few more days. An attorney stood up and announced, "I think I can make it back, besides if we don't do something, we'll all die anyway!"

As soon as he stepped into the water and began to swim, the sharks swam towards him. As they reached him, instead of tearing him limb from limb, they lined up, two rows beside him and actually escorted him to and back from the ship. As he returned to the others, hauling a net of supplies with him, all the remaining passengers rejoiced.

"A miracle," they shouted.

"Not at all," said the lawyer, "merely professional courtesy."

78

The Yuppie

This young urban professional was opening the door of his new BMW, when another vehicle suddenly veered around the corner and hit the open door. The impact ripped it off the hinges and in moments the door and the other vehicle had vanished. The young man stood there astonished looking at his recently purchased prize in agonized helplessness. "My new car!" He cried, "My brand new car!"

The police arrived on the scene to find the hapless individual still whining about his ruined possession. "You yuppies make me sick," the officer berated him. "You're so worried about your precious car that you haven't even noticed that the impact ripped off your arm!"

The yuppie looked down, he turned white and screamed, "Where's my Rolex!"

79

The Zoo

Once upon a time there was this man that had been laid off from work. Of course, he was very qualified, but we all know how that goes today. He was off for months! He tried everywhere, but simply could not find work.

One day, he spotted a classified ad for "zoo workers, minimum wage, no experience necessary."

He thought, "Well, this is a little out of my line of expertise, but it sounds like it could be fun, no experience necessary and I am desperate!"

So the next day he went to the zoo and applied. They brought him in for an interview. After the personnel staff had asked him a few questions, they told him that they thought he would do nicely. When could he start?

He was startled, he had been without work for so long and they were now offering him the job on the spot. "Hold on just a moment," he said, "you haven't even told me what the position is!"

"Well," the personnel director replied. "You see, our gorilla died the other day and with all the federal cutbacks and such it is impossible for us to afford to get a new one. We were looking for someone to wear this gorilla suit on gorilla island and simply move around and act like a gorilla. Can you do it?"

At first, he thought not. But then, hey, he needed the money and it could be fun.

The next day he reported for work. He donned the suit and went off to the gorilla island. The first couple of hours, he just sat there quietly, not really knowing what to do. A few children started calling out to him and he looked up. He made a face and a loud grunting noise and a quick movement, and the children jumped back from the edge of the island. He was amused.

He became more animated and as he moved about more and more, a crowd began to gather.

There was a swing rope and he began to swing wildly back and forth, grunting and making wild noises. The people were amused and he was having a great time! He loved it!

Late in the day, he was swinging way around on the rope, he was getting tired and he suddenly lost his grip on the rope. He was way up in the air and he came down in the next island, the lion's island!

He fell with a ker-plunk. He lay there stunned briefly, and as he looked up he noticed the lion sitting across the island under a tree. The lion's head was raised, and he was watching.

He jumped up and went to the wall and started jumping, trying to reach the top. Of course, it was out of his reach.

He continued to jump and as he jumped the lion stood up and began to walk towards the gorilla costumed man. The man jumped more and more and began to shout out, "Please! Help me!"

The lion began to run as the man shouted for help and continued to jump as best he could.

The lion ran faster and faster, getting closer and closer. The man jumped and jumped and was screaming, "Help! Help!"

The lion reached him and said, "Hey, pipe down, will you? We'll all lose our jobs!"

80

Those Swinging Seniors

A group of seniors were traveling by train on a special tour offered by their town's local travel agency. As usual, there were a great many more widows and just a few widowers.

While sleeping soundly in the upper birth, Mr. Anderson awakened to a persistent tap, tap, tap, tap from the birth below him. "Mr. Anderson," came a quiet voice from the widow below, "are you awake?"

"Now I am," he answered sleepily.

"It's rather chilly down here," the widow whined, "would you mind getting a blanket for me?"

"I've got a better idea," Anderson replied, "why don't we pretend, just for tonight that we're married?"

The woman giggled softly below him. "That sounds like a simply delightful idea," she suggested invitingly.

"Good," Anderson said as he rolled over, "go get your own blanket."

<u>81</u>

Three Englishmen

There were these three Englishmen touring the countryside in a convertible sports car. The engine was running full out, the top was down and the wind was blowing in their ears.

As they passed through a small town, one of the men shouted, "Isn't this Wembley?"

"No, it's Thursday," said the second man.

"So am I," said the driver. "Let's stop for a pint of ale."

82

A True Story

The teacher was having a parent / teacher conference with the parent of one of her newest students. The parent inquired, "How was "little Johnny" doing?"

The teacher responded, "Academically, he seems to be doing fine, but he seems to have a lot of trouble relating to the other students, his maturation is not as developed."

The parent said, "Well, you know, I home *teached* him for three years."

83

Two Ancient Kingdoms

There was, once upon a time, two neighboring kingdoms. The kingdom of Oshgosh, and, to the north lay its rival kingdom Ohmigosh. These two kingdoms had been at war for many years. So long in fact, no one remembered why. It had been a bitter feud and throughout the years many had been killed on both sides.

The kingdoms were separated by a strong, wide and flowing River. The only way across was a small drawbridge that had been built centuries past. This bridge could be used to travel from kingdom to kingdom and, in fact, it was the only way, as the River was so intense.

Decades before, the ruler of Omigosh had hired a pair of gigantic yellow fingers to protect its borders from any Oshgosh raiders. The fingers had patrolled the waters along the draw-bridge successfully, fully protecting Ohmigosh's borders.

A new king came to rule Oshgosh, he was a kindly man and a fair man. A man with high virtues. He saw no need for the feud to continue. No one could remember what had started it, anyway. He composed a letter to the neighboring kingdom, a letter that was diplomatic in all senses and affirmed honor for both kingdoms. It would work to lay the foundation for many prosperous treaties and trade agreements.

He sent for his most trusted minister. "Please," he said, "Take this across the River and deliver it to the king of Ohmigosh. It is time that our quarrels end."

The minister immediately set forth. Unfortunately, the giant yellow fingers, the protectorates of Ohmigosh could not distinguish between good men and evil. As the minister crossed the bridge, they came up from the deep, they plucked him from the bridge and held him under the water until he was dead.

The king was saddened when he heard the news. The tragedy made him even more determined to end the long standing feud. He sent his second minister. The same fate befell him. A third, who met his death. A fourth who then joined his predecessors. The king was not discouraged and he sent forth his entire cabinet until no one of importance was left in his court. They had all fallen prey to the giant yellow fingers.

He called for his page. "Young man," he beckoned. "Yes, sire," the page replied. "Young man, take this document across the bridge to the king of Ohmigosh," the eager leader commanded.

The page was horrified. He was familiar with the ends of his seniors and the thought of the giant yellow fingers caused a quaking in his boots. Alas, he went forward. He reached the kingdom's edge and nervously began to cross the dangerous threshold. The fingers shot up from the deep, but then, they remained motionless until the page had crossed into the land of the Ohmigosh.

The ruler of Ohmigosh was amazed at the young leaders persistence. He read the document and declared that they would make peace with their neighbor. Everyone lived happily ever after.

The moral: Let your pages do the walking through the yellow fingers.

84

Young Father Mally

Young Father Mally had just been ordained and was about to hear his first confessions. He asked Father Martin if he would listen in and critique his handling of the assignment because he was anxious to get his ministry off on the right foot.

At the end of the day the two clergy sat down and reveiwed the proceedings of the day.

"You did quite well," Father Martin said. He then hesitated, making sure that he would make his comment most appropriately. "However," he added, "in the future, you might want to make more of an effort to say, 'I understand' instead of, 'Oh, wow!'"

John Irvin

John Irvin, and his wife Cindy, are the co-creators and owners of Lifestyle Enhancement Services (LES), a successful motivational and consulting business.

LES offers keynotes, seminars and workshops that are designed to enhance conferences, conventions, annual meetings, trainings and special events. In fact, LES will make any meeting a special event!

John holds a degree in Recreation Administration from the University of Tulsa. He has been active in creating "playful opportunities" for personal and professional development for over twenty years. Today, as president of Lifestyle Enhancement Services, and creator of Hilarity Therapy® Programs, John shares from his work in corporate training, leisure sciences, mental health, and health & wellness education the message that each of us has the ability to enjoy life more.

John says "all work and no play make Jack (& Jill) suicidal!"

John Irvin is a member of the American Association for Therapeutic Humor, the National Speakers Association, the Oklahoma Speakers Association, the American Society for Training & Development, the Humor and Health Institute, the Association for Experiential Education, Project Adventure, Inc., and the International Jugglers Association.

For more information on John Irvin and his programs contact:

Cindy Irvin, P.M.S.
(Professional Marketer of Spouse)
Lifestyle Enhancement Services
Post Office Box 4397
Tulsa, Oklahoma 74159-0397

888-997-PHUN
or e-mail us at
jmi1953@ionet.net